AROUND THE WALLS OF
POMPEII

THE ANCIENT CITY
IN ITS NATURAL ENVIRONMENT

edited by Annamaria Ciarallo
and Ernesto De Carolis

ELECTA

**250th anniversary of the beginning
of the excavations at Pompeii
1748-1998**

This itinerary was financed
by the European Union under
Objective I - Measure 5 -
"Cultural tourism"

*Cover: A. Guesdon, Pompéi,
Vue prise au dessus de l'Odèon
et du Théâtre tragique*

© 1998 Ministero per i Beni Culturali e Ambientali
Soprintendenza Archeologica di Pompei
Published by Electa, Milano
Elemond Editori Associati

This tour of the ancient walls of Pompeii provides a view of the site that will surprise even those who think they know it well. But it is only one of the many secrets that Pompeii hides in its bosom. There are many other aspects that are totally ignored, either because they are difficult to understand or because they have not yet been brought to public attention and are waiting for their moment of glory.

The Soprintendenza Archeologica of Pompeii has drawn up a schedule of projects to promote a wider knowledge, if not of all of Pompeii, at least of more than what is open to visitors at present. This schedule will take some time to be completed and, at the end, although some of Pompeii's secrets may have been unveiled, new riddles will probably spring up to tease our intelligence.

What we are offering to visitors coming to Pompeii from all over the world is a mere piece of a mosaic buried and preserved by the eruption of the Vesuvius and much ravaged by the neglect of men. An effort is necessary now to bring order and harmony to the site. This requires the cooperation of many and the attention and participation of all, especially of those who come to this ancient city, be it for a short tour or an in-depth visit. Our work would be useless if those who visit the site did not respect it and help to keep it clean and tidy. The Soprintendenza Archeologica offers to all this new tour of Pompeii's natural and archaeological attractions as a symbol of a new pact with those who will spend some of their time here, in the hope of returning again.

Pietro Giovanni Guzzo
Archaeological Superintendent of Pompeii

A CITY AND ITS TERRITORY

Pompeii's territory after 79 A.D.

If an ancient Pompeian could have flown over his territory, he would have appreciated in full its extraordinary beauty praised by the writers of his time. The imposing bulk of the Vesuvius, whose volcanic origin was unknown at the time, rising in a large cone much taller than today, dominated the plain through which the Sarno river flowed lazily. The plain was bordered on the seaside by a long strand of sand dunes giving way to extensive marshes near the delta of the river.

Pompeii stood on a hard lava hill rising above the black sand of the nearby beaches. The river lapped its east side. The residential villas of Stabiae, built on cliffs overlooking the sea, dominated the gulf. Vineyards climbed up along the slopes of the Vesuvius, and woods capped its summit.

The eruption of 79 A.D. greatly transformed the area, burying the ancient cities as well as their woods and fields. Two thousand years from then, the landscape can be reconstructed from ancient literary and iconographic sources, as well as the study of organic remains found in the soil such as wood, pollen, seeds, animal bones, or solidified impressions of ancient plants. In the light of all these data, it is possible to picture ourselves on a trip through the ancient Vesuvian territory.

1. The Vesuvius in the fresco of the lararium of the House of the Centenary. Notice the single-cone shape of the volcano. Naples, Museo Archeologico Nazionale

Those who came from the sea landed on beaches with dark sand, bordered by pine groves mainly composed of Aleppo pines *(Pinus halepensis)*, sea pines *(Pinus pinaster)* and nut pines *(Pinus pinea)*, all of which had considerable importance in the local economy, as they yielded the resin used to coat the inside of wine amphorae. If one landed near the mouth of the Sarno river, to reach land it was necessary to make one's way through marshes thick with reeds and bordered by willows, poplars, ashes and alders. The reeds *(Arundo donax* or *Phragmites australis)* were widely used in building to make skillfully assembled lattices on which plaster was applied.

Left of the mouth of the Sarno, the dunes and the land behind the dunes merged with salt quarries. Salt was an indispensable ingredient of *garum*, a widely exported fish sauce, and was also traded inland along the navigable course of the river. The Sarno had very limpid waters, abounding in fish, where the *Anodonta cygnea* prospered (a large edible bivalve mollusk with a beautiful mother-of-pearl shell). Its waters were channeled to irrigate the fertile fields of the plain. Along the bends of the river one attempted to reclaim cultivable land from the marshes, the kingdom of wading birds. Land reclamation was done by planting cypresses arranged in a quincunx, whose mineralized trunks were found in several places. The fertile territories of the plain, especially the plots just outside Pompeii, were planted with vegetables for the daily supply of the town market. Depending on the season, lettuce, broccoli, onions, cauliflower, broad beans and peas reached the table of the ancient Pompeians. Plants needing fresh soil were also cultivated in the plain. They included hemp and linen, whose stalks were retted in the water of the river, and brooms, which at the time were widely used to make textiles. Vines were also grown in the plain, generally interspersed with poplars to preserve them from the humidity of the soil. Herds of cattle grazed on the marshiest land. As one began to climb the slopes of the Vesuvius, vineyards became the dominant feature of the landscape, as a painting in an ancient lararium shows us. They alternated with fruit orchards and grain fields, oats, wheat and barley being the most common species. Among fruit trees, nut, hazelnut and walnut were preferred, as their products could be preserved for a longer time. Apple, pear, peach and apricot trees were also grown. Their fruits, when they were not eaten fresh, were preserved dried or dipped in honey. There were beehives just about everywhere. Since both cane and beet sugar were unknown, the most common sweetener was honey, sometimes replaced by the sugary meat of figs.

The sunny countryside was dotted with "rustic villas", i.e. rural houses of varying size, depending on the size of their estates. Sometimes they were actual country residences with sumptuous rooms for the owner and his family and ample slaves' quarters. The most renowned villa of this type is the Villa dei Misteri, which lay at a short distance from Pompeii. Judging from the size of the room where wine was made, its surrounding estate must have been quite vast.

As one climbed higher, the fields gave way to oak groves, sometimes fenced in to raise pigs in a half-wild state and thus allow them to mate with wild boars to bear offspring with especially choice meat. The oak groves then gave way to beech groves, the reign of red and roe deer, a coveted game for local hunters. Only on the summit of the moun-

tain did some barren and difficult to access plateaus betray the mountain's volcanic origin.

The arc of the gulf was concluded by the long calcareous range of the Lattari mountains. The inhabitants' deep knowledge of the characteristics of the different types of soil guided them in their choice of crops. Thus, the calcareous terrain of Mount Faito was reserved to olive trees, as the numerous oil presses found there attest. The Lattari also offered excellent grazing grounds for the transhumance of numerous flocks from the plain to the mountains. Sheep and goat cheese was produced in great quantities, and there was a flourishing wool commerce centered round Pompeii.

The resources of the territory were thoroughly exploited in the town as well as the countryside. Trees rising above the high walls of *viridaria* betrayed the presence of gardens hidden inside the houses. On the

2. Philological reconstruction of the green areas of Regio II. Here it is possible to picture to oneself the ancient Vesuvian landscape. The only difference is that the Vesuvius has two cones

outskirts of the city, near the amphitheater, there was a quarter, mostly inhabited by people of modest means, that was being radically renovated. Here, green spaces were used in a different way. There were intensively cultivated vegetable gardens, and on some of the larger properties perfumes were produced, or fish raised in tanks. Young trees were grown, especially hazelnuts, which were then sold to be transplanted in small urban orchards. Rich Pompeians took advantage of the extensive open spaces in this peripheral quarter and of the availability of running water from the aqueduct to create fruit-tree orchards and large gardens or parks opening onto the outside.

Such were the Vesuvian landscapes and gardens of 79 A.D. They reflected a harmonic relationship between man and his environment.

[A.C.]

The ancient city

The continuous eruptions of the Vesuvius through the centuries and the great urbanization of its surrounding territory make it difficult to provide a reliable reconstruction of the Vesuvian landscape in Roman times. It is certain, at any rate, that the city of Pompeii was built on a high lava spur, the furthermost branch of an ancient lava flow of the Vesuvius. It was not far from the coast; and the buildings between Porta Marina and the suburban Villa dei Misteri all overlooked the sea. This nearness to the sea and to large salt quarries, as well as the river Sarno (at whose mouth there was an active fluvial port) were certainly a decisive factor in the economic and cultural prosperity of the city which, in Roman times, became an important and wealthy commercial center on the road between Naples and Nocera.

According to tradition, Hercules founded Pompeii as he was coming back from Iberia after de-

3. D. Anderson:
Porta Nolana and
entrance to the
excavations, silver
bromide print, ca. 1920
(private collection)

4. Unknown:
The Triangular Forum,
albumin print from a
collodion plate, end of
the 19th century
(private collection)

feating Geryon and seizing his famous oxen, and gave the city its name after leading the animals there in a triumphal procession ("*pompa*"). Actually, such mythical foundation tales exist for every city of the ancient world. The most recent archaeological investigations have revealed that the earliest urban nucleus of Pompeii was built around 600 B.C. by local populations, the Oscans of the classical literary tradition. Later on, during the 6th and part of the 5th century, the city, like other large and small towns of Campania, fell within the Greek and Etruscan political and cultural sphere of influence. According to some interpretations, the name of the city derives from the Greek noun *"pompeion"*, meaning "expedition" and stressing Pompeii's very early commercial inclination.

By observing the plan of the city and carrying out deep soundings in several points, it was ascertained that the most ancient urban nucleus occupied the southwestern part of Pompeii. However, at that time the walls already surrounded the entire volcanic plateau, and their perimeter remained the same throughout the life of the city.

5. G. Sommer:
The Forum, albumin
print from a collodion
plate, ca. 1870
(private collection)

This early town, extending from Porta Marina to the Triangular Forum, had a surface of about ten hectares. It had an irregular street network delimiting small blocks, and two sanctuaries—one dedicated to Apollo, the other to Hercules or Minerva—in an area which, at the time, possibly lay outside the city, and was later occupied by the Triangular Forum.

Around the end of the 5th century B.C., Pompeii came under the influence of the Samnite populations of the inland regions, who expanded rapidly, occupying the entire region of Campania. Their arrival marked the beginning of a new age for Pompeii, which became an important trading center and witnessed an increase in population leading the city to expand over the plateau. The new quarters were laid out according to a regular orthogonal plan with rectangular blocks delimited by the intersections of the *decumani* (east-west streets) and *cardines* (north-south streets), which connected to the street network of the earlier urban nucleus.

In the 4th century B.C., new migratory waves of Samnites from the Apennines swept down upon the urbanized and wealthy peoples of the Campanian plain. Rome also took part in the endless series of wars that followed (343-290 B.C.), after the Samnites of Capua asked it for help, and eventually became the dominator of Campania. From this moment onward, except during the interlude of the Carthaginian invasion during the second Punic war (218-201 B.C.), there was an economic and building boom in the region. From the first half of the 2nd century B.C. onward, Pompeii also enjoyed a period of great prosperity, reflected in the sumptuousness of private residences, such as the House of the Faun, the renovation of earlier public buildings and the construction of new ones, such as the Basilica and the Temple of Jupiter.

When the Italic cities joined forces against Rome in the Social War, Pompeii took sides with the other Campanian cities in their struggle to obtain the political rights deriving from Roman citizenship. In the month of April of 89 B.C., the Roman army, led by Lucius Cornelius Sulla, after seizing Herculaneum and Stabiae, besieged Pompeii, forced it to capitulate and occupied it. A few years later (80 B.C.), Sulla himself, to reward with land the veterans who had fought for him, founded a colony here. He called it *Colonia Cornelia Veneria Pompeianorum*, naming it after his tutelary goddess who thus became the patron of the city.

From the 1st century B.C. onward, the history of Pompeii was the same as that of other prosperous cities of the Roman province. Its wealth continued to be founded essentially on the trading of the products of its territory, such as wine, oil, wool and *garum*, the famous fish sauce used to season foods. According to Pliny the Elder (*Naturalis Historia*, XXXI, 94), Pompeian *garum* was one of the best in the Empire. The city extended far beyond its walls, now obsolete, and eventually became a typical Roman town, with squares, public buildings and a dense connective tissue of shops, ateliers and houses of various size and refinement, depending on the wealth of the owners.

In 62 A.D., a violent earthquake, almost an omen of what was to come, interrupted the industrious life of Pompeii, damaging many buildings so badly that part of the population was forced to quit the city. The eruption of Vesuvius in 79 A.D. spelled the end of Pompeii, of nearby Herculaneum and of the villas of Oplontis and Stabiae.

The emperor Titus, having been informed in Rome of the catastrophe, nominated a senatorial committee to bring succor to the survivors and assess the magnitude of the damage in view of a possible reconstruction of the city. The attempt was useless. Pompeii was almost totally buried by volcanic material, while Herculaneum had completely vanished. The eruption had been too destructive to leave any hope of rebuilding the cities as they were before the disaster.

[E.D.C.]

6. Ed. Inalterabile:
*House of the Centenary,
silver bromide print, first
decades of the 20th century
(private collection)*

7. G. Brogi:
*House of Pansa, albumin
print from a collodion
plate, ca. 1880
(private collection)*

DOMVS CN ALLE
NIGIDI MAI

The evolution of the landscape

The eruption of August 24th, 79 A.D. greatly altered the geomorphology of the Vesuvian area. The quantity of material erupted
by the volcano was such that the course of
the river Sarno was moved eastwards, the
coastline was advanced, forming the present-day Stabian plain, valleys were filled in,
and new hillocks appeared. The volcano it-
self was reshaped, acquiring a second summit.

The entire area was practically abandoned.
It was resettled in a sporadic but diffused
fashion in the 2nd century A.D., when na-
ture's continuous cycle had made fertile
again part of the sterile eruptive soil. Farmers recommenced to grow vines and cereals,
although from time to time new eruptions
reclaimed part of the cultivated land.

The locals continued to lead a relatively
peaceful life until the 7th century A.D.,
when continuous barbarian incursions first,
and then many even more fearsome Saracen
raids led again to the abandonment of the
Vesuvian plain which in a few decades was
overrun by immense forests reaching from
the coast to the summit of the volcano,
while the land along the banks of the Sarno
river became increasingly marshy. These
woods, especially the Sylvamala and the
Woods of Scafati, are recorded in Anjou reg-
isters as royal hunting grounds, while the
marshy areas were used for the cultivation of
textile plants, especially hemp. A protocol of
King Ferdinand of Aragon (1458-1494)
records the vastness of these woods that
reached all the way down to the coast, and
extended northwards to Nola, westwards to
Torre del Greco and eastwards to San
Marzano, interrupted here and there by
small groups of rural houses clustered
around a monastery.

It was Alphonso II of Aragon (1494-1495)
who first realized that it was no longer possible to reserve that entire territory for
hunting, with all the accompanying inter-
dictions, and sold part of the estate. From
that moment onward, the landscape began
to change, first slowly, then at a quickly increasing pace. Woods were cut down and
new farming settlements appeared as new
territories were reclaimed by agriculture. At
the beginning of the 17th century, the hill
slopes were mainly planted with vineyards
and cereals. There were numerous farms
served by "botteghe, maccaronerie, forni e
da chianche" (shops, macaroni factories,
ovens and butcheries). The increase in population of the nearby city of Naples created
a demand for new services and a higher
productive output. Thus, the count of
Sarno resolved to deviate the waters of the
river towards Naples around 1650, to allow
mills to be constructed on the outskirts of
the city. He eventually decided to direct the
waters to the nearer town of Torre Annun-

8. G. Gigante:
Gates of Pompeii (private
collection). Notice the
festoons of grapevine
supported by the trees
and the Arcadian setting
of the scene

ziata instead, which thus increased its importance as a milling center. This new hydraulic regime clashed with the needs of count Celano, who in 1629 had built some unauthorized sluice gates in Bottaro to supply his own mills, thus causing many plots of land to turn to marshland, and drawing upon himself the anger of local farmers. This situation gave rise to a dispute that lasted decades, and led to extensive hydraulic works made useless by a violent eruption in 1631 which brought destruction and death to the area, and put a stop to the mills' activity. In 1648, as the canals were being restored, a violent flood silted them up again. The rebellions led by Masaniello were the last straw: the mills were definitively abandoned. A few years later, in 1653, a terrible cholera epidemic broke out. The number of victims was enormous. Naples and its agricultural hinterland, which depended on commerce with the city for its existence, were depopulated.

At any rate, it was these hydraulic works of the 17th century (sometimes entrusted to renowned engineers such as Domenico Fontana) that brought to light, for the first time, some remains of ancient Pompeii. Those canals are still visible in some points of the archaeological area, e.g. near the Large Gymnasium and in Via di Nocera. A few years after the cholera epidemic, a cadaster map showed the location of the ancient Pompeian "theater" near the tavern "del rapillo," which at the time stood at the edge of the woodland. It was actually the amphitheater, whose site was known as "Scudella" ("bowl") from the bowl-shape of the buried building.

In the second half of the 18th century, under Charles of Bourbon, the Vesuvian landscape was again greatly transformed. This king undertook systematic excavation of

9. A. Guesdon, *Pompéi:
Vue prise au dessus de
l'Odèon et du Théâtre
tragique* (private
collection). This splendid
image, a reworking of a
picture taken from a
montgolfier, shows the
territory between
Pompeii and the sea.

Notice the scarce
urbanization, the Regia
Strada delle Sicilie on
the left, the steam-engine
train heading for Torre
Annunziata, the crater
of the Somma enclosing
the cone of the Vesuvius
in the background, in
the foreground the

excavations with, on the
right, the Casina
dell'Aquila

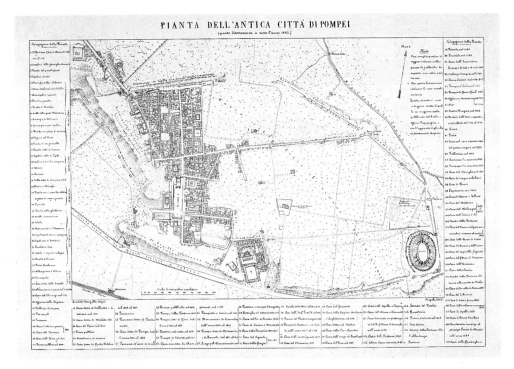

PIANTA DELL'ANTICA CITTÀ DI POMPEI
(quanto Sotterrata a tutto l'anno 1845)

the site of Pompeii and built a new royal palace in Portici. Thus, the Neapolitan nobility discovered the charm of the Vesuvian coast and began to build their summer houses there, along a stretch of road later known as the "miglio d'oro" ("golden mile"). Thus, the urbanization of the east coast of the gulf began, also favored by tax exemptions.

In the same period, a gunpowder plant originally lying just outside the gates of Naples was moved to the old mill buildings of Torre Annunziata, where a cold steel factory was also installed, while spinning mills were set up in Sarno. Thus, the first industrial towns were established in the Vesuvian plain. The spinning mills had a decisive impact on the landscape, as they gave a boost to cotton production and the cultivation of mulberry trees for the rearing of silkworms.

Visitors taking the Road of the Two Sicilies to visit the marvels brought to light in the excavations crossed a landscape interspersed with huge poplar trees, yellow with wheat fields in the summer and white with fluttering cotton-seed pappi at the end of autumn. Rows of grapevines, sometimes supported by trees, sometimes by reed or chestnut poles, stretched out along the lower slopes of the Vesuvius. The boats of fishermen and coral hunters floated lazily on the sea. Along the banks, reed lattices sheltered the fields from the salt carried by the wind.

In the distance, thin wisps of smoke, a sign of the presence of charcoal-burners, drifted above the thickly wooded Lattari mountains. On the terraces of the pasta factories overlooking the sea, pasta left out to dry swayed in the saline wind. One could catch river eels and crayfish in the limpid waters of the Sarno, which at the time was still navigable.

Pompeii, which was just beginning to be brought to light, was part and parcel of this landscape. The diggers worked in the shade of poplar trees and vineyards, flocks invaded

10. B. Marzolla:
Plan of the ancient city
of Pompeii, Naples 1845
(private collection).
The "collinette di lapillo
provenienti dagli
scavamenti" ("mounds of
lapillo from the
diggings") are marked
along the perimeter of
the excavations

its ancient streets, women sat chatting on the high sidewalks. Many pictures of this period highlight the Arcadian peacefulness of the site, which is also stressed in the descriptions of travelers. Along the edge of the excavations overlooking the sea were artificial hills, the so-called "cumuli borbonici", made of the lapilli dug up to bring to light the ancient buildings.

Latapie, a cultivated French traveler, looked with worry upon grapevine cultivation on the still unexcavated part of the site, rightly fearing that deep hoeing could damage the immediately underlying walls, but he was ahead of his time. To his contemporaries, it mattered little if, after a few decades, the recently excavated areas were overrun with spontaneous vegetation: their romantic souls took great delight in ruins overgrown with bramble.

At night, the ancient merged with the modern in the flashes of light of the still occasionally erupting volcano. Leopardi wrote: "*And in the horror of the secret night/ over the empty theaters/ the warped temples and the broken/ houses, where the bat hides his offspring/ like a sinister torch/ wandering dismally among uninhabited palaces/ sweep the flashes of light of the funereal lava, glaring red from afar through the darkness/ and tingeing the surroundings.*"

In the second half of the 19th century, new factors altered the Vesuvian landscape again. A terrible phylloxera epidemic wrought great and, in some respects, irreversible damage on the local vineyards. Another epidemic struck the dark mulberries, causing a fall of silk production and hence dealing a hard blow to the spinning mills of Sarno. Both of these events had a great impact on the landscape. Vineyards were replaced by fruit-tree orchards (locally grown peaches and apricots were especially good), and mulberry trees by ailanthuses, a symbiont of the *bombix,* in the hope of saving the silkworms. Unfortunately, the *bombix* never adapted to Italian climate, while the ailanthuses caught on so well that they became a weed.

11. A. Pisa:
Tomb with a
semicircular seat,
watercolor. Peach and
apricot trees have
replaced the vineyards
and poplars previously
characterizing the
landscape

The crisis of the Sarno spinning mills and land reclamation works undertaken along the entire basin of the river led to the abandonment of the cultivation of textile plants and the conversion of the plots to vegetable gardens.

The "Schito vegetable gardens" became famous for their artichokes and the entire Sarno plain for its San Marzano tomatoes. Phylloxera also destroyed the vineyards bordering the excavations. The latter were finally beginning to be regarded as a patrimony to be safeguarded. Latapie's views were eventually espoused, and the state appropriated the land enclosed by the walls of the ancient city, allowing only grazing upon it. The growing of vegetables within the perimeter of the walls was allowed again only a few decades ago. In the meantime, modern Pompeii was expanding around the excavations. The erection of a sanctuary of the Virgin Mary, drawing pilgrims from the entire region, also contributed to its development.

The harmonious integration of the archaeological area with its natural surroundings was short-lived. Studies carried out at the end of the 19th century ascertained that the local flora comprised about 1,000 species, not counting domestic plants. Some of the species found inside the excavations had never been described before. From the Fifties onward, an increasingly chaotic urban growth overran the fertile Vesuvian agricultural land. The fields gave way to closely packed houses, regardless of volcanic danger. Modern Pompeii has grown to a distasteful and threatening presence crowding upon the excavations. The peopling of the countryside and the use of chemicals to treat plants has led to the loss of about 300 species in a short time. It was only a few years ago that the Natural Park of the Vesuvius was instituted to preserve what remained of a much impoverished environmental patrimony.

Today, the Pompeian archaeological area, comprising 86 hectares of common land, half of which is green, is the largest park in the Vesuvian territory. It has also acquired a special naturalistic value, as it is a haven for many species ousted from the rest of the territory by the increase in population and the use of chemicals.

[A.C.]

12. A. Pisa:
The undiscovered city and the discovered city, watercolor. It shows the dirt road going through the fields along the edge of the excavated area, presently incorporated into the circuit of the walls. On the horizon are the great pines still bordering the path

13. Pompeii and the south side of the city. Until the Fifties, the public plots inside the excavations were used for grazing flocks

The rediscovery of Pompeii

The eruption of 79 A.D. changed the Vesuvian landscape radically. The economic life of the area was temporarily interrupted, and the survivors of the catastrophe moved to nearby towns. In the years immediately following the eruption, the roads were restored, but no large towns were established, and the diverse productive activities that had made the area so rich were not resumed. With the passing of the years, the higher parts of the buildings of Pompeii still emerging above the eruptive layer disappeared. The locals continued to dig the entire area of the town in search of precious or re-usable materials. In the centuries following the political and economic crisis of the Roman Empire, the memory of the site of ancient Pompeii was lost. The area where the city had stood acquired the significant toponym of "Civita," alluding to the masonry structures regularly encountered by farmers during agricultural work, or to the precious objects found by excavators.

One has to wait until the end of the 16th century for the first precise report on the discovery of ancient buildings in the area. The architect Domenico Fontana, while digging a canal issuing from the river Sarno, stumbled upon frescoed walls and marble decorations which, however, he did not attribute to the lost city. Of his contemporaries, only Giulio Cesare Capaccio, discussing these finds, identified "Civita" as the site of ancient Pompeii.

About a century later, in 1689, more walls and some inscriptions were found during the digging of a water well. The inscriptions were shown to the Neapolitan architect Francesco Picchetti, who attributed them to a villa of Pompey the Great. A few years later, a Veronese called Francesco Bianchini rightly disputed Picchetti's interpretation and attributed the inscriptions to the city of Pompeii. His hypothesis was later confirmed by Giuseppe Macrini, after the enlargement of the well led to the discovery of further vestiges of the ancient town.

Nevertheless, systematic exploration of the site only began in 1748 when, in the wake of the sensational discoveries in Herculaneum, Charles of Bourbon undertook a series of extensive and continuous excavation campaigns directed by the Spanish military engineer Roque Joachim de Alcubierre, who was assisted first by Karl Weber and then, from 1764 onward, by Francesco La Vega. Initially, the site was excavated haphazardly,

to the main purpose of finding precious or at least especially beautiful objects to grace the royal collections and draw the admiration of illustrious guests visiting the Kingdom. Thus, excavation concentrated on areas where one could descry the outline of large structures. The buildings brought to light in this early phase included the *Praedia* of Iulia Felix, the Villa of Cicero and the Porta Ercolano (Herculaneum Gates) with the Via dei Sepolcri.

When Francesco La Vega took over, a new page of the history of the excavations was turned. La Vega excavated more organically by concentrating on areas of limited extension to make at least part of the city accessible to visitors. Thus, excavation was carried out along the Via dei Sepolcri, where the monumental Villa of Diomedes was brought

to light, and on the south side of the city. Here, the excavation was extremely successful, leading to the discovery of the Large Theater, the *Odeion*, the Triangular Forum and the Temple of Isis. The decorations connected to the mysterious world of the Egyptians found in this last building caused a sensation.

La Vega's project of eventually joining the two excavation areas was achieved only during the Napoleonic decade (1806-1815), thanks to the work of Antonio Bonucci who, in 1812 and 1813, brought to light the Forum with its administrative and religious buildings, including the Basilica, the *Macellum* and the Temple of Apollo. Caroline Bonaparte, wife of Joachim Murat, was the main sponsor of the excavations in this period and endorsed a plan to bring to light the entire city. All the plots overlying Pompeii were acquired by the State. To delimit the excavation area, one began to unearth the entire perimeter of the walls, only a few short stretches of which had been excavated up to then.

This large-scale project could have been achieved only by concentrating considerable human and economic resources over several years. Instead, it was prematurely interrupted by the fall of the Napoleonic sovereigns

14. G. Brogi:
Via dei Sepolcri,
albumin print from a
collodion plate, ca. 1880
(private collection)

15. G. Brogi:
Villa of Diomedes,
albumin print from a
collodion plate, ca. 1880
(private collection)

and the return to Naples of Ferdinand of Bourbon. During the following years, however, the excavation extended to the northern areas. In 1824, one discovered the Forum Thermae, the first thermal facility brought to light, and the crossroads of Via della Fortuna and Via di Mercurio.

In the following years, a series of brilliant and unexpected discoveries were made: the House of the Tragic Poet, a complex of refined houses on Via di Mercurio and finally, in 1830, the house of the Faun (Goethe's son, Augustus, attended its excavation), with its exquisite mosaics including the famous representation of a battle between Alexander and Darius. All these sensational finds and the endorsement of Francis I of Bourbon (1825-1830) gave a considerable impulse to the investigation of the site in the last years of the Kingdom of the Two Sicilies.

The Direction of the Excavations of Pompeii continued to dig along the Via della Fortuna-Via di Nola axis in the direction of the Porta di Nola, up to the crossroads with Via di Stabia. The latter was unearthed up to the crossroads with Via dell'Abbondanza. Thus, the north part of the city (*Regio* VI and V) was finally connected to the Theater area (*Regio* VIII).

The discovery on the Via di Stabia, in 1847, of the House of Marcus Lucretius, with its small garden graced by marble statues and refined wall frescoes, caused a sensation. It was regarded as the most important house found up to then, after the house of the Faun.

A fundamental stage in the history of the excavations was the birth of the Kingdom of Italy. Under the new government, Giuseppe Fiorelli, a famous Neapolitan archaeologist, was appointed to Director of the Excavations. Fiorelli's methods were completely innovative with respect to the past. Besides ap-

plying the revolutionary technique of digging one horizontal layer at the time in homogeneous sectors, Fiorelli gave adequate consideration to the necessity of recording and drawing what was discovered. To facilitate the identification of the buildings, he adopted the system, still in use today, of subdividing the city into *Regiones* (quarters) and *Insulae* (blocks) with street numbers.

Fiorelli is also credited with the invention of the method of pouring molten plaster in the cavities which diggers had been finding in the ash since the beginning of the excavation of Pompeii. These cavities turned out to be impressions of vanished bodies and objects. This technique, first applied in 1863, provided startling images of the victims of the eruption. In 1875, Fiorelli's Pompeian activity was concluded when the Ministry of Public Instruction, Ruggiero Bonghi, called him to Rome to put him at the head of the newly instituted Direzione Genrale delle Antichità (General Direction of Antiquities).

In the following decades, there were increasing efforts to make the vast archaeological area of Pompeii accessible to visitors. Excavation went on, leading to the discovery of important buildings, such as the House of the Centenary in 1879-80, the House of the Silver Wedding in 1884 (dedicated to the sovereigns of Italy, Umberto I and Margherita of Savoia), the House of the Vettii with its exceptional frescoes, in 1894, and finally, in 1910, the extraordinary Villa of the Mysteries. Research advanced further under the supervision of Vittorio Spinazzola, a brilliant Neapolitan scholar who, between 1911 and 1923, resumed excavation on a large scale, concentrating his investigations on the south part of the city. Spinazzola brought to light the entire Via dell'Abbondanza, the most important street of Pompeii, connecting the Forum with the Amphitheater. The operation was a surprising success. It revealed a previously unknown Pompeii, full of life and color, with vividly colored signs painted over shop entrances, representations of deities in the "popular" style, and electoral propaganda painted on the walls of houses. The accuracy of the excavation methods employed made it possible to reconstruct with more precision than before the upper stories of houses, which were found to have been

16. G. Brogi:
*Temple of Isis, albumin
print from a collodion
plate, ca. 1880
(private collection)*

17. G. Brogi:
*Gladiator School,
albumin print from a
collodion plate, ca. 1880
(private collection)*

graced by balconies, galleries and verandahs overlooking what must have been the most busy and lively street in Pompeii. From 1924 to the Sixties, the Direction of the Excavations was held by Amedeo Maiuri, a fundamental figure of Italian archaeology, the last to undertake large-scale excavation campaigns inside the city. Initially, he focused on the *insulae* overlooking the south side of Via dell'Abbondanza. Spinazzola had only brought to light the facades of the buildings, without digging inside them. Maiuri continued to unearth the *insulae* of the *Regiones* I and II, proceeding from west to east, until the important discovery, between 1933 and 1935, of the Large Gymnasium. Inside this structure was an impressive number of Pompeians killed in the last phase of the eruption during a desperate attempt to flee along the road connecting Pompeii to Nocera. The most sensational find in this sector was the House of the Menander, excavated between 1927 and 1932, one of the most noble and refined Pompeian houses, which yielded a famous silverware service presently in the Naples archaeological museum.

In 1929-1930, the excavation of the suburban Villa of the Mysteries was resumed and completed. In 1933-34, the walls of Pompeii were almost entirely revealed, bringing to completion a job begun but never achieved by the French. Finally, from 1953 onward, the monumental necropolis of Porta Nocera was brought to light. Underground stratigraphic soundings were carried out, providing important information for the reconstruction of the historical and urban phases of Pompeii. These data are still very useful today.

As the excavation campaigns went on, large-scale restorations were also undertaken. The *tribunal* of the Basilica, the columns of the Forum and the portico of the Large Gymnasium were re-erected. The house of the Menander was completely restored. The roofs of many houses were rebuilt to provide better protection for their pictorial and sculptural decoration. To maintain a realistic image of the city, the decoration and ornaments, when possible, were left *in situ*, and the gardens and fountains were restored. Maiuri carried out in-depth studies and maintained an unequaled attention to the outward appearance of the city. The period

of his supervision was the most fruitful and innovative in the history of the excavations. From the Sixties onward, excavation campaigns became less frequent. Only the monumental houses with several stories of the *Insula Occidentalis* and the House of Iulius Polybius in the *Regio* IX were unearthed. All energies were concentrated in an attempt to avoid the slow deterioration of the city, to be able to hand down to future generations the unparalleled result of 250 years of research. [E.D.C.]

18. Aerial view of the amphitheater, silver bromide print, early 20th century (private collection)

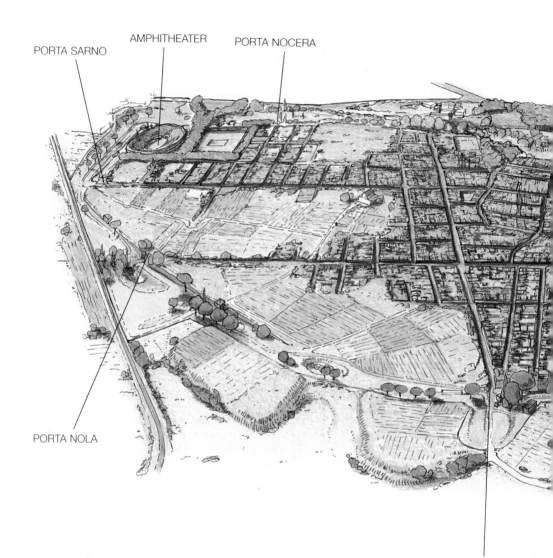

PORTA SARNO   AMPHITHEATER   PORTA NOCERA

PORTA NOLA

PORTA VESUVIO

The itinerary is about 3,000 meters long. One begins at Porta Ercolano, on the west side, goes eastwards passing Porta Anfiteatro and finally reaches Porta Nocera. To make things easier for the visitor, the itinerary has been subdivided into three laps of approximately the same length. The path mostly runs on the Bourbonic mounds in front of the walls,. regaining the ancient ground level near the entrance gates and the roads issuing from them, flanked by necropolises. Thus, visitors walk most of the time on high ground, and can thus see the ancient city from above and take in the surrounding landscape

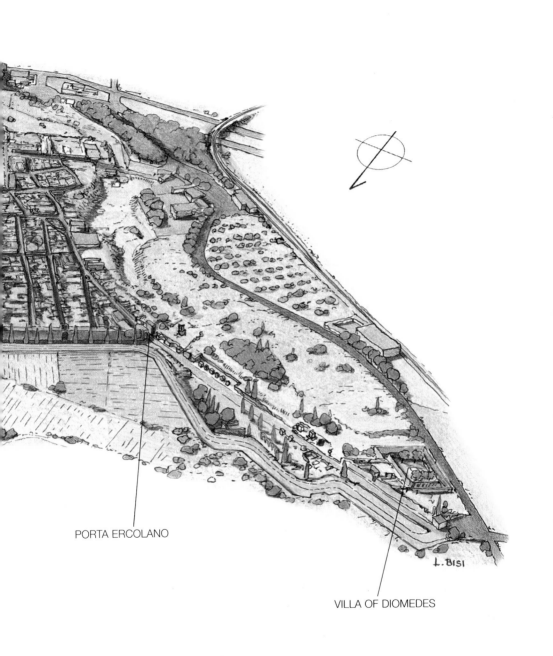

PORTA ERCOLANO

L. BISI

VILLA OF DIOMEDES

FROM PORTA ERCOLANO TO PORTA VESUVIO

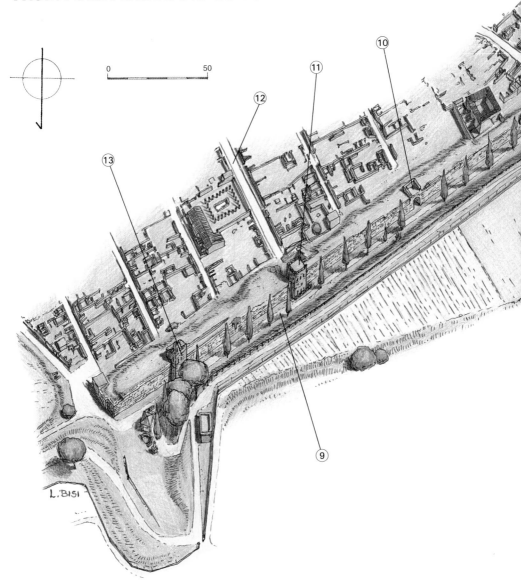

0   50

L. BISI

1. Tomb of Aulus Umbricius Scaurus
2. Villa of Diomedes
3. Villa of the Mosaic Columns
4. Stopping area
5. Porta Ercolano
6. Tomb of Marcus Cerrinius Restitutus
7. Tomb of Mamia
8. Tomb of the *gens Istacidia*
9. *Pomoerium* road
10. Tower XII
11. Tower XI
12. Via di Mercurio
13. Tower X

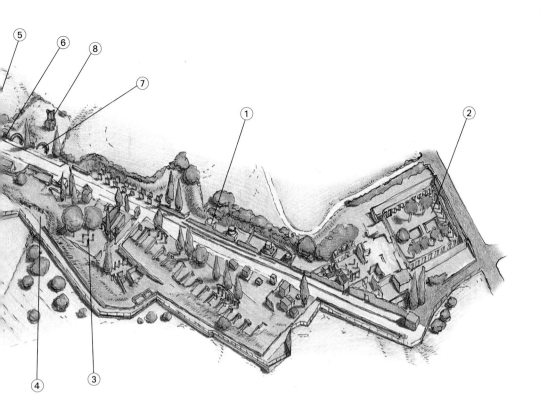

To reach the summit of the pedestrian path, it is necessary to walk up a slope rising slightly above the present-day ground level, a material token of the thickness of the layer of pyroclastic materials erupted by the Vesuvius in August, 79 A.D. As one goes up, the view on the right is interrupted by two elders sporting large white umbels in the springtime.

The necropolis of Porta Ercolano was the first to be explored systematically between 1763 and 1814. Numerous funerary monuments were brought to light, mostly datable between the foundation of the Sullan colony and 79 A.D. A small group of trench inhumations of the Samnite period (4th-3rd century B.C.) was found in the area of the Villa of the Mosaic Columns. The most diffused burial ritual in the Roman period was incineration. The ashes were generally stored in earthenware, marble or glass urns placed in niches.

From where we stand, we see an altar tomb on a high stepped podium belonging to Aulus Umbricius Scaurus, the member of a wealthy *gens* who produced *garum,* the famous fish sauce. Then comes an elegant cylindrical tomb on a rectangular podium and the tombs of Gaius Calventius Quietus and Naevoleia Tyche, surmounted by altars with dosserets.

A monumental suburban villa opens onto this stretch of the road. It was excavated between 1771 and 1774, and was arbitrarily attributed to the emancipated slave Marcus Arrius Diomedes. From our observation point, we can see the *prothyrum* and part of the peristyle. A group of Pompeians sought shelter from the fury of the eruption in the cryptoporticus (underground corridor) of the villa. Their bodies were found in 1772 in a layer of volcanic ash, and caused a sensation.

On the left of the road, going towards Herculaneum, one passes a long row of shops preceded by an arched portico fronting the Villa of the Mosaic Columns, whose long entrance corridor gave direct access to a garden with an irregular plan containing a nymphaeum (a monumental fountain) with a mosaic niche. At the center of the garden were four columns faced with mosaic that gave the villa its name. They are presently in the Museo Archeologico Nazionale in Naples.

A bit further along the path, after passing a cluster of holm-oaks, one reaches the first halting place, where some cypresses and a beautiful plane tree occasionally hide from sight the splendid view of the Stabian gulf, the Villa of the Mosaic Columns, and the Porta Ercolano on the left.

Outside of the monumental triple-arch gates of Porta Ercolano (the side ones were for pedestrians), one encounters on the left the tomb of the *augustalis* Marcus Cerrinius Restitutus, with a low vaulted niche flanked by seats, called "garitta" ("sentry-box") in 19th century descriptions, as the body of a man wearing a helmet was found here. Moving on, one passes two exedra-tombs of Nocera tuff, ending with winged lion paws. The first belongs to the *duovir quinquennalis* Aulus Veius, the second to the famous priestess of Venus

19. View of the Tomb of Mamia and that of the Istacidii

20. Beginning of the itinerary. In the foreground, elders in blossom; on the left, cypresses and holm-oaks

Mamia, whose family (one of the most influential of the Augustan age) boasted close ties with the imperial family. Behind her grave is a tomb consisting of a high podium surmounted by a circular aedicule, some of whose columns are preserved. It belonged to the *gens Istacidia,* and does not overlook Via dei Sepolcri, but a side street descending steeply, possibly towards the nearby ancient littoral. Here, adjoining Via dei Sepolcri, is a hillock planted with vegetables. It is artificial in origin, being made of the lapilli dug out of the ancient houses of Pompeii in the Bourbonic period. Such mounds are commonly known as "cumuli Borbonici" ("Bourbonic mounds").
Beyond the hillock, on the horizon, Capri emerges from the sea. It seems to be joined to the Punta della Campanella, i.e. the extremity of the Sorrento-Amalfi peninsula, the final stretch of the range of the Lattari Mountains. The island was truly part of the peninsula until a sinking of the earth was filled in by the sea, separating it from the mainland. The blue profile of the calcareous Lattari Mountains rises up to the top of Mount Faito, whose summit

is still capped with thick woods. At the foot of the Faito, the Stabian plain stretches out. It is formed of the alluvial deposits of the river Sarno and the pyroclastic projectiles hurled by the Vesuvius. It is here that the naturalist Pliny the Elder died during the eruption of 79 A.D. His nephew, Pliny the Younger, described the tragic events of those days in two letters to the historian Tacitus. The densely populated plain reaches down to the sea, where one can descry shipyards. On the right are the houses and port of Torre Annunziata, and ancient Oplontis, where two monumental villas buried by the eruption of 79 A.D. were discovered.
The rock of Rovigliano is clearly visible out at sea, with the ruins of a castle that gave the city of Castellammare its name. The Romans called this rock *Petra Herculis.* The legend has it that there was a temple of Hercules here to watch over seafarers, as well as some other buildings probably belonging to a villa. In the Middle Ages, the temple was transformed into a monastery that remained in use for quite a long time, until the 15th century, when it

was renovated and converted to a watchtower. It is the ruins of this last phase that are visible today on the rock.
From above, we look down on the *pomoerium* road, devoid of sidewalks and paving, a stretch of consecrated ground where building was forbidden, running along the external perimeter of the walls, like in Rome and its other colonies. It can be reached by a right-hand detour skirting the most significant stretch of the Pompeian walls. This stretch was excavated only partially in 1811-1812, and was soon covered up again by landslides and weeds. It was definitively brought to light, together with the *pomoerium* road, by Maiuri in 1933-1934, as part of a never completed project to unearth the entire perimeter of the walls.
The outside walls, which were already partially interred during the last years of Pompeii, show different chronological phases:
Phase I: sectors made of travertine orthostats (vertically arranged blocks), some of which were laid horizontally into the earthwork at regular intervals to reinforce the structure (first half of the 5th century B.C.);
Phase II: sectors of *opus quadratum* made of travertine blocks laid parallel and perpendicular to the wall (4th century B.C.);
Phase III: sectors of Nocera-

21. Porta Ercolano

22. Tomb of the Istacidii. In the background, the Sorrento peninsula, the arc of the gulf and the rock of Rovigliano

tuff *opus quadratum* (last decades of the 3rd century B.C.);

Phase IV: sectors of lava-stone *opus incertum*, datable to the years immediately preceding the Social War (end of the 2nd century B.C.-beginning of the 1st century B.C.).

Three towers of lava-stone *opus incertum* were inserted in this stretch of the walls. They are faced with white stucco imitating regular courses of rectangular blocks (First Style). Seven tuff gutters for the discharge of rainwater are still visible.

After passing a stretch of tuff *opus quadratum* with quarry marks incised on the blocks and the remains of the first tower (No. XII), one walks along a stretch of the walls built of lava *opus incertum* with some courses of travertine *opus quadratum*. Beyond the ancient city, the densely urbanized plain of Nocera and Sarno comes now into full view. At the center is a swarm of houses descending from Gragnano to Castellammare. On the left are the belfry and dome of the sanctuary of the Virgin, built in the first half of the 19th century to house a local religious tradition that goes all the way back to the cult of Pompeian Venus.

At the top of the path, which winds its way over one of the Bourbonic mounds surrounding the ancient city, we can appreciate in full the effects of the eruption of 79 B.C. on the landscape. The ground where we stand is on a slightly higher level than the crest of the walls on the right. The ancient ground-level lies, on average, 7-8 meters below, while we are only slightly above the cultivated fields on our left. On the left, we can also get a full view of the Somma-Vesuvius range, formed of the sunken part of the Somma (caldera), the more ancient crater, and the volcanic cone of the Vesuvius, which sprang up at its center. To picture ourselves the approximate height of the volcano before the eruption of 79 A.D., we should prolong its sides with imaginary lines up to their intersection point.

The towns of Boscoreale and Boscotrecase are well visible on the slopes of the volcano. In Roman times, many rural villas were built in this area. Some were actually country residences decorated with refined frescoes in the sector reserved to the master's family, e.g. the villa of Publius Fannius Synistor and that of the Pisanella, where one discovered a famous silverware service, presently in the Louvre. In the foreground are typical crops of the Vesuvian area. Orchards, mostly of peach and apricot trees, are interspersed with vegetable gardens that prosper on the ex-

Via di Mercurio

From the tower, our gaze embraces a large sector of the city crossed by the wide and elegant Via di Mercurio, which goes from the homonymous tower to the intersection with Via della Fortuna, on the left, and Via delle Terme on the right, and ends with an opus latericium (brickwork) honorary arch called "of Caligula" after a bronze equestrian statue whose vestiges were found here. Some of the most elegant and refined Pompeian houses open onto this street, including the House of the Dioscuri, the House of Meleager, the House of the Small Fountain and the House of the Large Fountain.

Brooms

Brooms (*Spartium junceum* L.) are the most characteristic plant of the Vesuvian landscape. They are the pioneers of the resurgence of plant life after the eruptions of the volcano. When the lava flows cool down, they are first colonized by a lichen, *Stereocaulon vesuvianum* L., exuding acids that begin to crumble the rock and thus pave the way for superior plants, first of all the brooms. The roots branching out from the brooms' seeds wedge in the cracks in the rock and then begin to grow, eventually disintegrating it until it pulverizes, becoming a soil suited for more demanding plant species. This process lasts hundreds of years. In May and June, the slopes of the Vesuvius are yellow with the brooms that colonized the 19th-century lava flows.

traordinarily fertile soil. Broad beans, peas, tomatoes, eggplant, pepperoni, cabbage, cauliflower, broccoli and lettuce are grown, each in its own season. There is also a great local tradition of floriculture. On the right, along the slope, are specimens of *alaternus* and some brooms whose trunk-like stalks betray their old age. Rows of cypress trees occasionally conceal the rampart and the streets of the ancient town. We now reach the central tower, No. XI, called "of Mercury". It has two stories with loopholes above the ground floor and a passage leading to the patrol walkway on the crest of the walls. Inside the tower, staircases roofed with barrel vaults run along the walls, turning at right angles. Under the tower, Maiuri found a stretch of the most ancient walls of Pompeii, made in the first half of the 6th century B.C. with a local rock called "pappamonte." Tower X and a magnificent pine conclude this lap of the itinerary. This last tower was reconstructed in all its height by Maiuri, on the basis of the excavation data and the vestiges of the original structure, which are delimited by a red-brick border to distinguish them from the restored part. Some circular holes are still visible in the walls on the left of the tower. They are the marks of stones hurled by war machines during Sulla's siege of Pompeii in the Social War. The walls are well preserved here, and it was thus possible to reconstruct them quite faithfully.

23. Spartium junceum L.

24. Via di Mercurio

In the most recent phase, the walls, which ran for 3,250 meters along the edge of the lava spur on which Pompeii was built, had an external and an internal wall curtain, both fitted with merlons about one meter high, presumably added in the 3rd century B.C. to defend the patrol walkway. The external wall curtain was much lower than the internal one. Behind the latter was an earthwork with bulwarks. The twelve towers arranged at regular intervals were added in the last phase of the Social War. Their counterclockwise numbering, beginning from Porta Stabia, was gleaned from Oscan inscriptions painted in several locations inside the city during the Sullan siege to direct the movements of the defensive troops. The walls had seven gates, to which, as in the case of the streets, modern conventional names have been attributed: Porta Ercolano, Porta Vesuvio, Porta Nola, Porta Sarno, Porta Nocera, Porta Stabia, Porta Marina. (The existence of an eight gate, dubbed "Porta Capua," has also been suggested.)

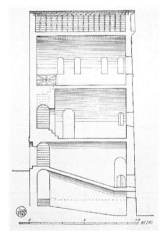

25. Tower of Mercury

26. Tower of Mercury, front view. Reconstruction by A. Maiuri from a 1943 drawing by Oliva

27. Tower of Mercury, cross-section. Reconstruction by A. Maiuri from a 1943 drawing by Oliva

28. Stretch of the fortified walls. Reconstruction by A. Maiuri from a 1943 drawing by Oliva

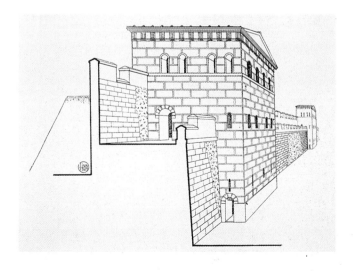

FROM PORTA VESUVIO TO PORTA NOLA

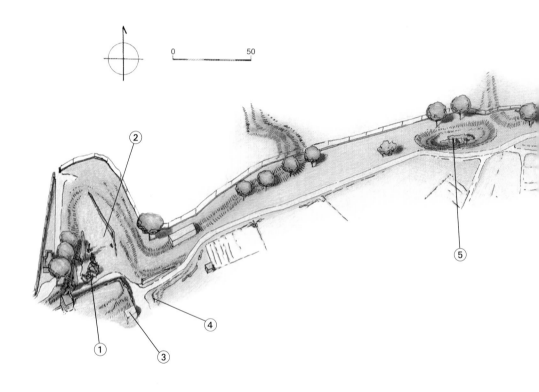

① Tomb of Gaius Vestorius Priscus
② Cippus of Titus Suedius Clemens
③ *Castellum Aquae*
④ Lararium of *Insula* 6, *Regio* V
⑤ "Excavation of the Japanese"
⑥ Tower VIII
⑦ Stopping area

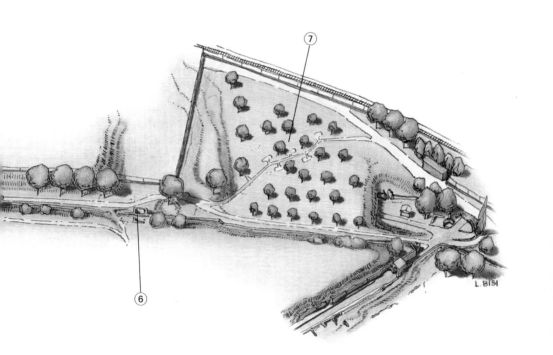

L. BISI

The necropolis of Porta Vesuvio, shaded by planes, cypresses and a gigantic pine, lies along a road probably leading to the volcano. A few tombs delimited by lava-stone blocks, probably part of a larger necropolis, were brought to light in this suburban area. The most conspicuous tomb is that of Gaius Vestorius Priscus. It is a masonry structure composed of an enclosure with four pinnacles at the corners, surrounding an altar with pinnacles on a high podium leaning against the north wall of the enclosure, with four additional small altars at the corners, connected by a concave wall. Above these small altars are snakes of painted stucco. The entrance doorway lies at the center of the west wall of the enclosure. Both the main altar and the small altars are also decorated with stucco Maenads, Satyrs and Erotes. A marble slab on the east side of the altar commemorates the erection of the tomb by Mulvia Prisca for her twenty-two year old son Gaius Vestorius Priscus, who held the office of aedile. Nearby are a masonry enclosure-tomb, an exedra-tomb ending in winged lion paws, with an ungrooved column at its center, and a tomb with a tuff column on a high podium. On the other side of

29. "Roverella" oaks growing on the walls

30. Necropolis of Porta Vesuvio. In the background, a pine near Tower X; in the foreground, the Castellum Aquae

the road is a travertine cippus with an inscription recording that the military tribune Titus Suedius Clemens, by decree of the emperor Vespasian, was charged with evacuating the strip of public soil outside the walls after it had been illegally occupied by private citizens following the earthquake of 62 A.D.

Further along the path, after walking on a short stretch of the ancient pavement, one reaches the remains of the gates, which collapsed during the disastrous earthquake of 62 A.D. and were never rebuilt. On the right is a stretch of the

walls made of blocks of Nocera tuff. It joins the *Castellum Aquae* built on the highest point of the city. The water brought by the Augustan aqueduct was conveyed inside this structure, from where it was distributed throughout the city by means of a network of lead pipes. At this point of our itinerary, our gaze embraces *Insula* 16 of *Regio* VI (where the remains of a house with a wall decorated in the 1st Style are visible) and Via Vesuvio, with the House of the Golden Amorini and the House of the Ara Maxima. After climbing back to the

modern ground level, the path runs shortly along the inside curtain of the walls made of travertine orthostats, the only stretch of the fortification of the 5th century B.C. still well visible today.

On the right, on a corner of *Insula* 6 of *Regio* V, we can admire a lararium painted on the wall to protect the street intersection. It features a central altar flanked by two agathodaemon snakes, bringers of good luck and fertility. *"Agathodaimon"* was the Greek name of the Egyptian god *Khnum*, who was represented as a snake hiding in the two caverns from which the waters that fertilized Egypt issued. In Greek mythology, he was later assimilated to another homonymous deity protecting the fields, the vineyards and the city, and thus became a typical element of Pompeian lararia. A proba-

bly later addition is a frame containing the inscription *"Cacator sic valeas, ut tu hoc locum trase(s),"* a playful appeal to relieve one's bowels elsewhere.

The walls then disappear from view under the fields overlying the part of the ancient city that has not been excavated yet. As we go on, vegetable gardens grown on public land extend on our right over the ancient streets and houses. Behind them we see the back of the Casina dell'Aquila, an 18th-century building owned by a homonymous family. Until the middle of the 19th century,

grapevines were grown in these fields, combined with poplar trees, a very ancient technique presently surviving only in some very small areas of the province of Caserta. Their cultivation was prohibited when one realized that the practice of the "scasso", i.e. deep hoeing and shoveling, while necessary for the growing of grapevine, damaged severely the underlying ancient buildings.

Beyond the fields interspersed with ancient poplar trees, where vegetables are grown intensively, the horizon is closed off by the long range of the Lattari mountains, rising on the right to Monte Sant'Angelo a Tre Pizzi, their highest summit, named thus after its three successive peaks, two of which are nicknamed the "canine" and the "molar" owing to their shape. The town of Gragnano, dominated by its castle, extends down the slopes of the mountains shrouded with woods mainly composed of coppice chestnut trees. Following the profile of the peaks towards the left, one descries the pass of Chiunzi, leading to Ravello and the Amalfi coast. Resuming our walk on the pedestrian path, we find on

31. Lararium painted on the wall at a corner of Insula 6, Regio V

32. Excavation of a stretch of the walls of Pompeii in the area where a "Porta di Capua" is presumed to lie

our left a stretch of the walls recently brought to light by the Japanese School of Archaeology, which reminds us again of the difference in height between the present and the ancient ground-level. There is a hypothesis that a still unexcavated gate of Pompeii, called "Porta Capua," lies in this area. Along the slopes and in the fields, several plant species flower, each in its own season. Some of them are rare.

Past the so-called "excavation of the Japanese", left of the slight slope leading downhill to a level halfway between the present ground-level and the one of 79 A.D., are two striking ancient specimens of Christ's-thorn (*Gleditsia triacanthos* L.), a tree of North American origin with very long and sharp thorns, probably brought here at the time of the beginnings of the excavation, or even earlier.

As we walks along the following level stretch, we admire an extremely engaging landscape dominated by beautiful umbrella pines. One proceeds along the ancient patrol walkway on the crest of the walls. Only one course of the external curtain emerges from the

ground. On the right, elm trees and oaks of a species called "roverella," a typical feature of the ancient landscape, of which they are a relic, throw their shadow on the inside curtain of the walls, made of travertine *opus quadratum*, of which only the upper part emerges from the ground.

A new rise brings us nearer to the ground-level of 79 A.D. On our right, inserted in a long stretch of the walls made of tuff *opus quadratum*, is a ruined tower (No. VIII) built of lava-stone *opus incertum*. Its white stucco facing, imitating

courses of *opus quadratum* blocks, is still preserved. The tower is collapsed down to the first floor. On its front wall are three small loopholes splayed out in a half-circle. Beyond the tower, we walk along a long stretch of the walls, made of tuff *opus quadratum* above courses of travertine blocks belonging to the 4th century B.C. phase.

On the left, an ancient rural house, the home of a family of shepherds, dominates an ample stopping area alongside the railroad. The area is shaded by poplars, maples, "roverella" oaks, elms and planes. A bit further off, some tall holm-oaks and Aleppo pines rise above the guardhouse.

Those who are familiar with the song of birds will be able to recognize many of the species nesting in the area, such as doves (which are very numerous), blackbirds, goldfinches, chaffinches and robins.

33. Tower VIII

34. Stopping area. On the horizon, the mountain range of Sarno

The flora

The flora of the excavations is extremely interesting. It includes indigenous species which have disappeared elsewhere in the area due to its intense urbanization and the indiscriminate use of chemicals to treat plants, as well as ornamental species introduced from elsewhere. The indigenous species include some rather common ones such as the broom (*Spartium junceum* L.), whose stalk sometimes grows to a trunk, the acanthus (*Acanthus mollis* L.) and, in the fields, a species of radish called "rapestra" (*Raphanum raphanistrum* L.), as well as some rare ones, such as the *Glaucium corniculatum* (L.) Rudolph, the *Iris foetidissima* L., the *Asphodelus tenuifolius* Cav. and some species of orchids.

The species introduced later, in different periods, include the tree of heaven, *Ailanthus* (*glandulosa*) *altissima* (*Miller Swingle*), which has become a weed, and the Christ's-thorn (*Gleditsia triacanthos* L.). The trees are also very interesting, not so much for their rarity as for their age. Besides the already mentioned *Gleditsia*, those that have grown to a great height include umbrella pines (*Pinus pinea* L.), Aleppo pines (*Pinus halepensis* L.), "roverella" oaks (*Quercus pubescens* L.) and holm-oaks (*Quercus ilex* L.), near Porta Nola, and planes (*Platanus occidentalis*) and cypresses (*Cupressus sempervirens* L.) near Porta Ercolano.

On the grassy slopes of the Amphitheater, the botanist Michele Tenore picked and described for the first time three species. He also informs us that, in his times, it was fashionable for tourists to pick flowers in the archaeological area in memory of their visit.

35. *Ulmus glabra Hudson*

36. *Raphanum raphanistrum L.*

37. *Echium vulgare L.*

38 . *Gleditsia triacanthos L.*

39. *Garden peas*

FROM PORTA NOLA TO PORTA NOCERA

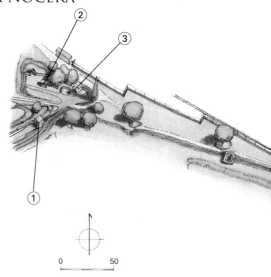

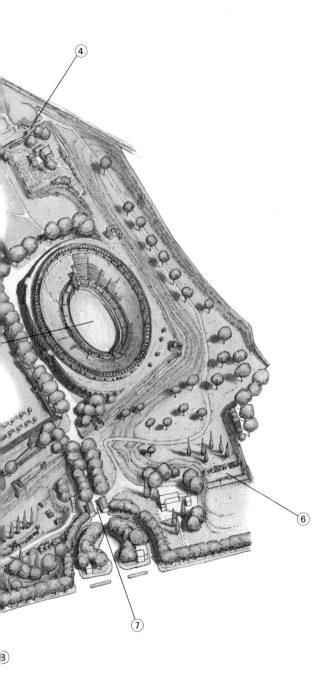

The necropolis of Porta Nola, as it appears today, looks remarkably like its representations in the lithographs of Piranesi. Possibly those who, at the beginning of the 20th century, landscaped the area for visitors drew inspiration precisely from Piranesi's images. Some large holm-oaks, a plane and a cypress border and throw their shade on the tombs. The exquisite pavement of the roads disappears under the still unexcavated pyroclastic stratum, giving a romantic allure to the scene. As we descend, on our left we see a large branch of the wide stone-paved road issuing from Porta Nola. This branch, which must have been important, also disappears under the pyroclastic flow of 79 A.D., whose section shows the wave-shaped trace of the last surge that definitively destroyed Pompeii. After the first rain of lapilli, a surge of extremely hot gas and ashes rolled at great speed down the slopes of the mountain, sweeping over those who, having survived the first phase of the eruption, were trying to escape from the city, as the bodies found in this area attest. On the right is Porta Nola. It is roofed with a barrel vault and protected by powerful bulwarks adjoining the city walls.

The stone-paved road descends quite steeply from the gates and branches out in several directions. One short excavated stretch skirts the wall, another seems to head towards the Nocera-Sarno plain. On the side of the road, a drain for the rainwater flowing down from the gates was found.

40. Exedra-tomb of Aesquillia Polla

41. Porta Nola

42. Tower VII

carried out in the area in 1908-1911 and 1976-1978, the bodies of 21 Pompeians killed as they were trying to escape from the city were unearthed. It was possible to make casts of most of them by pouring molten plaster in the cavity that had formed inside the hardened ash layer. The surrounding holm-oaks and planes were planted at the beginning of the 20th century, when they were already quite tall. Hence, some specimens are older than one hundred years. The slopes in front of the wall are decked with viburnum, myrtle and great tufts of acanthus and iris. The acanthuses, which grow spontaneously in the Vesuvian area, evoke the classical world, as the elegant volutes of their leafs were the inspiration for Corinthian capitals. The *Iris foetidissima*, one of the rare species of the flora of the excavations, has disappeared elsewhere, but has found a haven in the archaeological area.

From the ancient ground-level we walk back up to the present one through a thick grove of ancient holm-oaks. On the left, the path skirts the Circumvesuviana railroad, beyond which the east side of the Vesuvian plain stretches out, with the towns of Poggiomarino, Striano and, on the slopes of the Vesuvius, Terzigno. On the right, the upper part of the walls comes back into view. Another brief climb takes us back to the top of a still buried stretch of the walls. In front of us is the Sarno plain, bordered on the horizon by the mountains of Avella, where the source of the Sarno lies. This river was an important fluvial artery in Roman

Outside these gates, too, a small group of tombs was brought to light. The first one we meet is that of the aedile and duovir Marcus Obellius Firmus. The tomb, of the wall-enclosure type, is faced with white plaster and is fronted with a pediment containing a slab with a dedicatory inscription. At the center is a marker placed over the spot where the glass urn containing the ashes of the deceased was buried.

The next monument is an exedra-tomb of Nocera tuff with winged lion paws at its extremities. Behind and at the center of the exedra, on a high podium, is a Ionic column topped by a marble amphora surrounded by iron tridents to keep birds from nesting upon it. The tomb, as a marble slab tells us, was dedicated by Numerius Herennius Celsus to his twenty-two year-old wife Aesquillia Polla.

On the other side of the road is a tuff-exedra tomb, also featuring the two usual winged lion-paws at its extremities. Behind the exedra is a podium surmounted by an altar.

In the course of excavations

The finding of bodies

"On February 15th, 1863, while an alley was being cleared—called at the time Alley of Augustus, today Alley of the Skeletons—Fiorelli, the Director of the Excavations, was informed that the workers had found a cavity at the bottom of which bones could be seen. Inspired by a stroke of genius (although the idea was simple, nobody had had it before him), Fiorelli ordered work to be halted, had some plaster molten, and had it poured inside that cavity and in two more which had been observed nearby. After they had been filled up and one had waited for the plaster to dry, the crust of hardened pumice-stones and ashes enclosing the object of the search was removed with great care. After this envelope had been eliminated, four corpses appeared..." (E. Delaunay, Une Promenade à Pompéi, Paris 1877).

Delaunay described thus the invention of Fiorelli, which is still used today, and has made it possible to recuperate images of Pompeians frozen in the instant of their death in the final phase of the eruption, after the fall of the lapilli. This method can only be applied in the ash layer we find in Pompeii either on the ancient ground level, in buildings that were not invaded by the lapilli (e.g. in partially subterranean rooms), or at a height of about 3 meters, where its thickness is about 1.20 meters. The ash, by adhering to the bodies and various organic materials, such as wooden furniture, created a cavity preserving their form after they had naturally decayed.

43. Cast of a human body found by Maiuri during the excavation of the Large Gymnasium

The Vesuvius

The volcanic complex of Vesuvius-Somma was formed about 17,000 years ago. Until 79 A.D., eruptions of the Plinian type (i.e. explosive) followed one another at intervals of about 2,000 years, alternating with lesser eruptions. Pompeii was built on what was probably an obstructed magmatic crater. After 79 A.D., the activity of the volcano remained constant. There were numerous eruptions, fortunately not of the Plinian type. One of the most dramatic was that of 1631. A statue of St. Gennaro at the Ponte della Maddalena in Naples portrays the saint protecting the city, with his right hand raised to stop the lava. The activity of the Vesuvius stopped in 1944. Since that year, the plume of smoke immortalized in centuries of Neapolitan landscape painting has no longer been seen hovering above the volcano.

44. The Vesuvius viewed from the Pompeii-Sarno plain

45. Fight between the Pompeians and the Nucerians, fresco from Pompeii. Naples, Museo Archeologico Nazionale

46. The amphitheater of Pompeii

Amphitheater

The amphitheater was built at their own expense by the duoviri Gaius Quinctius Valgus and Marcus Porcius around 70 B.C. It is regarded as the most ancient known building of its type. It is elliptical in shape, and partially built against the earthwork of the town walls. On the side towards the city center are two double staircases supported by arches leaning against the outer wall of the building, providing easy access to the upper gallery. The other entrances included two single staircases and four long vaulted passages, of which the two extreme ones were paved to allow carriages to reach the arena. The vaulted passages intersected a corridor from which staircases placed at regular intervals led up to the stands (*cavea*). The *cavea*, as usual, was subdivided in a lower sector reserved to the authorities, and a middle and upper sector (respectively, the *ima, media* and *summa cavea*). It had seats made of stone, and could accommodate approximately 20,000 spectators. Large canopies were spread above the *cavea* to shield the public from the rays of the sun in the warmest hours. Gladiator shows were offered at their own expense by newly elected town officials or local notables. The gladiators were recruited among criminals and slaves, and were trained in schools (one of the most renowned was that of Capua).

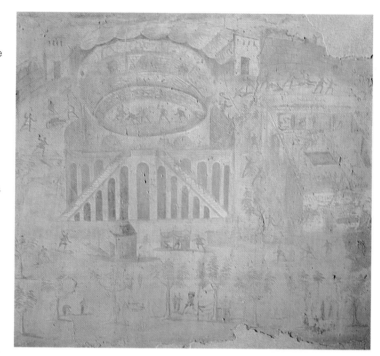

47. A stretch of the walls
near Porta Nocera

times, and its water was still limpid and navigable between the two World Wars. In the course of the centuries, its course was gradually deviated, first by the eruption of 79 B.C., then by a series of land-reclamation works that had a crucial role in the development of the intensive San Marzano-tomato farming industry supplying innumerable canning industries until a few years ago.

The path descends down to the Sarno road near the homonymous gates (Porta Sarno), of which few vestiges remain. We are now again on the ancient ground-level. On the left-hand slope are a hawthorn shrub and a few specimens of elder, relics of the original spontaneous vegetation of the spot, which has now given way to a small pine grove. On the right, the

imposing walls meet the upper stands of the Amphitheater. In the 18th century, the Amphitheater was the only visible structure of ancient Pompeii. About a century and a half ago, a famous Neapolitan botanist, Michele Tenore, gathered some up to then unknown species inside it. In the Amphitheater, during a gladiator exhibition in 59 A.D., there was a famous fight between Nucerians and Pompeians, which is represented in a fresco. Following this riot, the Senate voted a ten-year ban on the celebration of games in the Pompeian arena.

The path leads on through a newly planted pine grove and runs alongside a group of cypresses casting their shade on six tombs found by Sogliano in 1886 in the Fondo Pacifico. They are an extension of the vast necropolis of Porta Nocera, excavated by Maiuri from 1953 onward. The tombs lie along the ancient road connecting Naples to

Nocera, which skirted the south side of Pompeii. A very important find was made here: an inscription attesting for the first time the presence of a *Pons Sarni*, i.e. a bridge over the Sarno river.

We leave the path now and, after crossing an alley flanked by holm-oaks leading from the present-day entrance into the archaeological area, we go down a staircase to the necropolis of Porta Nocera, extending along the southwest side of the walls, built of travertine *opus quadratum* and leaning against the lava spur.

The path is flanked by clearings interspersed with brooms and tall cypresses. On both sides are tombs exemplifying several types of Pompeian funerary monument:

1 – Enclosure tomb with a pediment facade. Age of Nero (54-68 A.D.). It is the burial of Gaius Munatius Faustus and his wife Naevoleia Tyche. The couple also

owned a cenotaph outside Porta Ercolano.

2 – Tomb of the late Republican age (2nd-1st century B.C.). It is fronted by an archway flanked by three niches on each side, surmounted by a second floor with eight more niches. In two of the niches, tuff busts of a male and a female are preserved, identified by the inscriptions below them as Publius Flavius Philoxenos and Flavia Agathea.

3 – Tomb of the time of Tiberius (14-37 A.D.), shaped as a monumental exedra faced with Nocera tuff slabs, erected on a rectangular podium. Its crown is missing. The inscription on the enclosure informs us that it is the tomb of Eumachia, priestess of Venus, who erected the homonymous building in the Forum.

4 – Tomb of the late Republican age (2nd-1st century B.C.). It consists of a high podium supporting a shrine shaped as a four-columned temple (prostyle tetrastyle). The columns frame three cellae containing as many tuff statues depicting a young armed man between his parents. The inscription mentions the names of the owners of the burial, Marcus Octavius and his wife Vertia Philumena.

5 – Tomb of the Augustan age (second half of the 1st century B.C.-first decades of the 1st century A.D.) consisting of a shrine on a high podium. The shrine contains three tuff statues, a female one flanked by two male ones. The burial belongs to Publius Vesonius Phileros, and bears an inscription warning passers-by: "*Oh passer-by, stop for a short while, if*

you do not mind, and learn what you should be wary of. One whom I hoped was my friend accused me falsely. In the court, by grace of the gods and due to my innocence, I was absolved from all accusations. May the slanderer be rejected by the Penates and the gods of the Beyond." .
We go back now towards Porta Nocera where, at the intersection of the road running parallel to the walls and the road descending from the gates, is a travertine slab bearing the same inscription we

already encountered outside Porta Vesuvio, commemorating the reclamation of the strip of public soil outside the walls. The itinerary ends at Porta Nocera, which we reach after passing through two imposing bulwarks adjoining the walls just before the gates.

48. Necropolis of Porta Nocera

49. In the middle of the road is the cippus of Suedius Clemens. In the background, Porta Nocera and a stretch of the walls

BIBLIOGRAPHY

Storia della Campania, Naples
1992-1998.

M. Borgongino, "La flora
Vesuviana del 79 d.C.", in
*Paesaggi e Giardini del
Mediterraneo,* Acts of the 3rd
Meeting, 3, Pompeii 1993,
pp. 115-140.

L. Capaldo, "La fauna Vesuviana
del 79 d.C.", *ibidem,*
pp. 149-160.

C. Chiaromonte Trerè, "Nuovi
contributi sulle fortificazioni
pompeiane", in *Acme* 6 (1986).

A. Ciarallo, *Orti e giardini
di Pompei,* Naples 1992.

A. Ciarallo, "Giardini e paesaggi
vesuviani del 79 d.C.
Descrizione e confronti", in
*Paesaggi e Giardini del
Mediterraneo,* Acts of the 3rd
Meeting, 4, Pompeii 1993,
pp. 37-43.

S. De Caro, "Nuove indagini
sulle fortificazioni di Pompei, in
*Annali dell'Istituto Universitario
Orientale di Napoli. Sezione di
Archeologia e Storia Antica* 7
(1985), pp. 75-114.

E. De Carolis, "Testimonianze
archeologiche in area vesuviana
posteriori al 79 d.C."
in *Archeologia Uomo Territorio* 16
(1997), pp. 17-32.

A. and M. de Vos, *Pompei,
Ercolano, Stabia,* Guide
Archeologiche Laterza, Rome-
Bari 1982.

A. Maiuri, "Studi e ricerche sulle
fortificazioni di Pompei",
in *Monumenti Antichi
dell'Accademia dei Lincei* 33
(1930), cols. 114-276, pls. I-XII.

A. Maiuri, "L'isolamento della
cinta muraria fra Porta Vesuvio e
Porta Ercolano", in *Notizie degli
Scavi di Antichità* (1943),
pp. 275-294.

M. Mariotti, "Contributo alla
conoscenza del paesaggio
vegetale dell'area di Pompei nel
79 d.C.", in *Paesaggi e Giardini
del Mediterraneo,* Acts of the 3rd
Meeting, 3, Pompeii 1993,
pp. 141-148.

T. Pescatore, H. Sigurdsson,
"L'eruzione del Vesuvio del 79
d.C.", in *Ercolano 1738-1988.
250 anni di ricerca archeologica,*
Rome 1993, pp. 449-458.

F. Zevi (ed.), *Pompei,* voll. 1-2,
Naples 1991-1992.

GRAPHIC AND PHOTOGRAPHIC SOURCES

1, 46: Soprintendenza
Archeologica di Napoli

2, 23, 26, 29, 35, 36, 37, 38,
39, 40: A. Ciarallo

8: from *Viaggio Pittorico nel
Regno delle Due Sicilie*, vol. 2,
Naples 1829

9: from *L'Italie à vol d'oiseau*,
Paris, ca. 1845

11, 12: from W. M. Mackenzie,
Pompei, London 1910

13: from A. Maiuri, *Pompei*,
Rome 1929

19, 20, 21, 22, 24, 25, 26, 27,
28, 30, 31, 32, 33, 34, 41, 42,
43, 44, 45, 47, 48, 49:
Fotografica Foglia s.a.s.

3, 4, 5, 6, 7, 10, 14, 15, 16, 17,
18: private collection

AROUND THE WALLS
OF POMPEII

Texts by
Annamaria Ciarallo [A.C.]
Ernesto De Carolis [E.D.C.]

Pier Fausto Bagatti Valsecchi was
the consultant for the landscaping
of the tour of the walls.

Illustrations by
Ludovico Bisi

Translation by
Federico Poole

Printed in 1998 on behalf of Elemond Spa
by Tipografica La Piramide, (Rome)